A Trick of the Light

Also by Nan Dalton

Poetry

Beachcoming
Gleaning the Seasons
A Trick of the Light

Fiction

Tansy
Tansy's Moon
The Ammil Child

A Trick of the Light

Collected Poems

Nan Dalton

TO JULIE
WITH THANKS
AND BEST WISHES.
Nan Dalton

First published in 2003
by Perry Meadow Press
12 Fairfield Terrace
Newton Abbot
Devon TQ12 2LH

This edition with revisions and additions published in 2013

ISBN: 975-0-9543196-0-1

Cover illustration by Liz Dalton and Jo Ward

Printed by Short Run Press Ltd, Exeter

'Poetry is the best words in the best order'

'It is the job of the poet to find the best words to
describe the things we all see and feel.'

Samuel Coleridge Taylor

Nan Dalton was born in Essex and moved to Devon in 1962. She has written poetry since 1983 and was first published in the *Western Morning News* (1987), *Otter,* new Devon poetry and *The Common Thread*, Mandarin (1989). She read as 'Poet of the Week' on BBC Bristol & West (1990).

Attending the Arvon Foundation Poetry Course at Sheepwash, North Devon, led to the publication of *Beachcombing* (1993) and *Gleaning the Seasons* (1996). 'Writing for Performance' at Arvon Lumb Bank, Yorkshire inspired readings with friends at local libraries and clubs.

Prize winning continued at the Library of Avalon (1994), Teignmouth Arts Festival (1996) which led to the formation of 'Quintessential' with Ian Maun, Claire Freer and Margo Aldridge, reading at Newton Abbot, Teignmouth, Dawlish and Torbay libraries and at 'Ways with Words' (with Stephen Lloyd) at Dartington (1998).

Prizes also at Ottakar's 'Poetry Day' (2001) and 'Poems by Post No. 5', Torbay Library Services and the *Acumen Literary Journal* (2004). Her first novel *Tansy* won the Peninsular Prize for Fiction held by the *Western Morning News* and Halsgrove (2002). *Tansy's Moor* (2005) and *The Ammil Child* (2011) followed published by Perry Meadow Press, who also published a collection of poetry *A Trick of the Light* (2003) republished *as Collected Poems* (2013).

Acknowledgements

My thanks to Judy Chard and Christine Green (Creative Writing), members of the Estuary Writers' Workshop, Anne Born, (poetry tutor), Arvon Foundation and Exeter Arts. Johnathon Clifford (National Poetry Foundation).

Audrey Woolley, Mary Prowse, Claire Freer and Margaret Oliver reading as 'Nan and Friends'. Ian Maun, Margo Aldridge, Claire Freer and Stephen Lloyd reading as 'Quintessential'.

Stella Watson (Mitre Books), Andrea Snape (Ottakars), Carol Ackroyd and Linda Roland Howe (Newton Abbot library). Doff Pollard (Arts Officer, Teignbridge), Jan Fricker and Sue Avery (Wright's).

Contents

From *Gleaning the Seasons*

From *A Trick of the Light*

Unpublished

Devon Is . . .

Not red like poppies
in a field of corn,
not a singing robin
in a Domesday hedge
nor weathered sandstone
walls of Totnes Church

But red like foxes
crossing Dartmoor heath,
sand the colour
of Teignmouth beach
the steep steep soil
under an autumn plough

And a herd of red
coated Devon cows.

Poems by Post No. 5 (2004)

Cuckoo Rock

Were you there on Cuckoo Rock
when the wind blew strong
from the sea?

Did you crush the heather
whorls
as you rode beside the leat?

Cool booted feet among
shadow fish
Under a dazzle of damsel flies

And talk of other times,
other places
With tongues dyed bilberry
blue?

Did you climb tor high the
granite rock
See brood mares run the
valley floor?

Did you touch my hand on
Cuckoo Rock
or was it the mist from off the
sea?

Western Morning News (1987)

Wolborough Hill

Shut in with ancient stone
cut from granite hills
mood distanced by valley
wood and field

June canopied with wild translucent bloom
pierced through with marbled angel wings
while high above larks sing and stone children
guard the ever young asleep beneath a silver moon

Shaded by yew and owl roost pine
soldier widow they lie as one
beneath mason's marks on weathered stone
Tom 1917 – Bess 1971

Erect amongst the marguerite and autumn cyclamen
an ivied vault holds Councillor John
his wife and son made rich by men
who fished and died for cod off Newfoundland

Still parish feet cross cobbled paths
and granite hills in storm and sun
stand witness to Man's birth
and death and sweet reunion

Stone Woman

Axe rang rose and fell
fell and rose Mohan's hands
bent supple yew into
virgin loom thong bound
at base and head

Thrum thrum thrum thrum
Shuttle flew weft to warp
warp to weft Small hands bled
palms split by rough spun wool
heather stained a mordant blue

A boy sits rocking
wicker cradle hand to foot
foot to hand longs for
the hunter's return
lets sheep stray
leaves day to myth

Thrum thrum thrum thrum
Stone woman works at the loom
all day weaves wool cloth
till shadow anchors neolith
leaves grain whole
ashes dead

Horn sounds and women run
each to her man stopped by
a bier of soft deer skin
Mohan's son grown to man
takes up axe and bow in a shout of grief

Thrum thrum thrum thrum
Stone woman stays at the loom
all night Stiff and cold
she wakes with the sun wraps
finished cloak around her love
seals it tight with a fine bone pin

New Age Tempest

Anne Katharine Charlotte Patch
died 1924 mourned and missed
by Tom and Jack who placed her here
on Wolborough Hill
beneath Oak's Down

Each winter's snows quilted
Tom's Anne and children made
toboggan slides above Oak's roots
which anchored hill to bank
at town's edge

New Age tempest roared around
the hill blasted shook
tore out Oak's heart
with iron hands

Anchorless Anne's grave gone
hurled fifty feet on a devil wind
which split stone cracked bone
scattered ash on Oak

Whose roots lay bare cold rings
exposed Axe rang a mourning
bell death tolled Oak's history
his age – two centuries and
fifty three

Ethiopia 1984–89

Nanghi sat under sun taut canvas
wrapped in Tigrean shamma of famine torn black
too weak to reach the water carrier
too slow to catch the life giving grain

Her eyes followed the new Messiah
who walked and raged amongst her people
sending a manstar mirror of skeletal images
to haunt the viewers of Western screens

Voyeur-like replete we watched in horror
the human harvest on the plains
saw Nanghi saved by the miracle worker
who brought to life her recurring dream

of children playing in her childhood compound
while women tended the shooting grain
Watched the rescue of Nanghi sole surviver
to carry the name of the Tigrean chief

Now revolution falls from the sky
a wall of war splits hope and
Western charities Five years on
we re-cut discs to ease our pain

Green Talk

Chop it down it's in'way
spoiling the view
causing too much shade

    It came from Dartmoor a century ago
    split from a berried rowan tree
    which sheltered a tinner in Swincombe Leat

Chop it down it's in'way
bringing roaming dog yowling cat
we don't want that

    Blown on a westerly caught in a
    thread of Tom Drewe's coat as he
    travelled by Combestone to Newton and back

Where we come from we like
things neat beside it
spoils' look of street

    Trodden underfoot in a pen of sheep
    carried uphill on a current of air
    falling to earth in the corner – there

Photosynthesis? Chlorophyll?
Stop people from getting ill?
Well I've never heard of that

Growing by a villa of Isambard Bassett
a railway man scenting the air on an April evening
Making a red berried autumn awning
guarding us gently while we sleep
its feathered foliage stands thirty feet

Alright alright love
there's no need to go on if that's
how you feel After all it's only a tree

NB. Isambard Kingdom Brunel built Newton Abbot Railway Station.
Bassett Loce are railway model makers.

Decoy Wood

'Danger keep out' the neat
sign says One step away lies
a marshy death while parallel
bars replace purslane and sedge

and tangled paths become jogging tracks
'Meet here at 9' the programme says
'your community guide will take you round'

My wood my once wild wood
my silver wood hill hung
in the lee above the pale
green sheen of winter corn

East Prawle

Sally, September, and ivy seeds ripen
feeding black and red admirals
in velvet wing cases, painting stone
boundaries in glossy green spirals
shielding our bridle path down to the sea

Sand shoes fit snugly in foot impressed places
stepping and tripping in a blackberry scramble,
Sunday walk changing to headlong peramble
through butterfly flitter and harvesting bee.

Plunging in seas of emerald and sapphire
becoming as one with tide and sea drift.
Sally runs laughing, clutching at samphire
eagerly seeking a key to the cliff.

Missing Person

Newspaper headline reports
John Brown factory worker
father of three on
the missing persons list

Media picture shows
blow dried Anne and lining
the settee Lee Kevin and Diane
Microphone necklaces crackle
and say how they've missed

John who ran from the sweatshop
of his life –
    computergamescreditcardsC.B.radio
    deepfreezemicrowavenightly video –
to search among his roots

checking marble runs cricket walls
snooker bars fishing pools looking
for his chums Calling in on Grandma
for a mash of tea where the smell
of roses and unused tobacco pipes

sent him running down the hallway
driving home through tortured night
till gentle hands drew him back
through the gate –
    thankGodyou'rebackKev'sbeenexpelled
    caughtsniffinggluedeepfreezehasblown
but we've taped all your favourite soaps

Newspaper headline reports
John Brown factory worker
father of three yesterday
returned to his family

Family Album

She remembered
Church Rd head height marked door
climbing a roof with summer cousins
flashback of panic at angry neighbours
hurtling swings flying hair

But was I around he asked

She remembered
Bantham beach its deep rock pool
rainbow shells salty lips making
castles with grainy sand running
from seas in wellingtons

But was I around he asked

She remembered
Easter and a frost covered tor
playing King of the Castle on
Belstone moor The pictures are
there for all to see

But was I around he asked

New pictures grow
in a frame of leaves
brown hair brown eyes stand
hand-in-hand as together
they weave fresh memories

Look Mummy it's me and you he said

Paying Guests

On Saturdays our red haired African
guest played Celtic airs
on a tape deck by his bed

Proud of Islay where his ancestors
were born migrant birds rested salmon leapt
waterfalls – a far off isle to Scotland's West

He told me a story again and again
of Afrikaans the Long Trek men and women
dying under an African sun survivors settling
at last at Wittwatersrand

Where his grandfather another red haired
man wrested a living from native backs
harvested tobacco on drying racks made
a fortune in Krugerrands

Last Saturday our red haired African
guest paid his rent and left leaving behind
a thistle painted stone and a right wing cutting
from Johannesburg wishing that Mandela was dead

The Colour of Summer

Charlie arrived with the first shoots in May
challenging night frosts to strip clean
green vines strung out in lines
    on the south facing bank of the house
    with a view of Haytor

Jack gritted his teeth took up the gauntlet
netting fast forming fruits driving off Charlie
who called as he ran
    from the south facing bank of the house
    with a view of Haytor

Bets were laid in the village odds on Charlie
to win as June threw a gold blanket of shimmering heat
    over the south facing bank of the house
    with a view of Haytor

August grapes hung in a glory of blue
a luscious bloom covered bower of fruit
waiting the day of gathering to come
    from the south facing bank of the house
    with a view of Haytor

September's short days brought a harvest
at dawn Jack stripped to the waist
Charlie watched from the lawn
    of the south facing bank of the house
    with a view of Haytor

December and friends passed through the door
as Jack brought red bottles from under the floor
the colour of summer trapped in glasses of wine
   from the south facing bank of the house
   with a view of Haytor

'A good year' they said and raised glass to lip
and Charlie's loud clatter set a seal on the day
as he strutted proud pheasant all purple and green
   on the south facing bank of the house
   with a view of Haytor

Bride Price

Frost spangled mares tail
lay thick as a carpet
as I stepped through a gap
in the gold oak fringed wood

New corn grew strongly
in rows marching upward
stopped by the wall
of St. Bernadette's convent

where Sister Angelica
fingered her rosary
counting hours days years
as they swiftly passed by

I thought of the night
of the women's group visit
feelings of peace
as we stood in the hall

Felt again the hand
of Sister Angelica
as she led us forward
through the sitting room door

The light in her eyes
as she touched precious keepsakes
stripped from young novices
giving themselves to their Lord

White coif reflected
in a glass encased relic
sleeve shard of Lourdes visionary
young Bernadette

Bells rang for Vespers
but still she stayed on
till I whispered 'Please hurry
the others have gone'

Her hand flew like a bird
to her bare wrinkled mouth
then like a girl
she ran from the room

How many novenas
did Sister Angelica say
for breaking the rule
of the nunnery bell?

Hospitality turned to ash
in my mouth as I counted
the bride price of Sister Angelica
hidden from life by an old convent wall

Rush Hour

Heatwave
left me
a juddering wreck
fighting traffic lanes
of escapees from
everyday stress

Ignoring
lead fumes
they stared
straight ahead
eyes glazed over
with weariness

Venturing
out in a daring
move dodging containers
from far off Spain
hooted back to
the pavement again

and then I saw it

zig-zagging
busily round
my head
a tiger hawk moth
black and white striped
reversing to red

Lifting my spirits
dazzling my eyes
with its brilliant colour
brushing my cheek
with powdery
moth scales and

then it was gone
caught in the slipstream
of a passing bus

The View From Here

London and streets
hide your familiar face
behind a facade
of memory's
leaves

Pretty girls rush past
not one wears the face
I seek dressed in charity
black with Doc Martin
booted feet

Gallery walls
flaunt nature's colours
freedom poplars
blazing stones
of Rouen Cathedral

Would Monet's ice floes
on the Seine
crack and melt
beneath your warm
appraising look?

Shadows lengthen
in poppy fields
shading your green eyes
from summer sun
at Argenteuil?

Monet's childhood scenes
take me to another cliff
where we picniced
by an old stone
hut

a palette away
from Normandy
You sketched
then said goodbye
with camera shots

wearing jeans
a baseball cap
I sombre in sandals
faded cotton
frock

I buy cards
in a gallery shop
you paint lilies
on a winter lake
light years away

from Monet's
garden
at Giverny

Alhambra, Granados

I am planting sweet smelling myrtle
to remind me of a castle in Spain
where barefoot Muslims kneel in prayer
and western cameras flash

violating soaring stucco walls
forbidden to human image yet
bearing the five beliefs of Islam
engraved in Arabic

Washing in snow fed fountains
supported by stone sculpted lions
symbolising mediaeval friendship
between servant Jew
and Arab master

Praying in red clay courtyards
ruled by the call of the Muezzin bell
men turned south to Mecca
women veiled and guarded stayed
hidden by a harem wall

Fasting from sunrise to sunset
in perfumed lamplit alcoves till
moonrise changed crimson
crenellations into shimmering
silver towers

Almsgiving to beggars outside
a Pomegranate gate atoning thirty
severed heads a royal adultery
to expiate

Pilgrimage sent Moors riding north
to hear the Koran spoken in
a Mosque built at Cordoba
of Roman columned remains

I am planting sweet smelling myrtle
to remind me of a castle in Spain
where barefoot Muslims kneel in prayer
and western cameras flash

No Escape From The Media

A knock
at the door
hunting dogs call
paid by press barons
media lords
close heeled
to disaster

A raid
on private places
penetrating deep
into anguished hearts
nailing tears
to microphone crosses

A setting up
of scenarios
into suffering
minute by minute
on the spot reporting
rape accident
abuse murder

A filling of
hungry news jaws
death by tea time
killed by yet another
terrorist explosion
the media has a lot
to answer for

People Like That

'People like that' she said
(passing George as he shuffled along
all he possessed in a black plastic sack)
should be tidied away
out of sight

    Not accepting his choice of a life
    free from Society's rules
    the restriction of walls
    doled out time

'People like that' she said
are best institutionalised
becoming a schizo
is way out of line

    Even when communities welcome George in
    money brings laws into play
    outlawing those for whom space is paid
    in favour of future owners unknown
    who may perhaps object

One in ten suffer broken minds not bones
If minds wore splints would attitudes change
and people like her no longer talk of
'People like that'?

Writers' Day – October '90

We've lost out on sleep
all night listening
for digital bleeps
in a state of excitement

Jill's bombing along
motorway ring road
small country byway
looking for 'Pagan Leys House'

Best suits leather shoes
peering about us
we seem to be first
as we travel the driveway

        Is that the husband?

We eye each other –
romantic fiction
wear frocks crime writers
silk blouses poets trousers

        Is that the hostess?

Thought she'd be older
Fabulous ear rings
down to her shoulder –
she's this year's top novelist

I do like this room
hostess Jane says she's
stripped down to the bed
hired chairs rather hard no bard

                              Pity as I'm one

Chairman's upstanding
calls latecomers in
Introduces first
speaker agent called Wanda

Husband writes *sci-fi*
she plots *who dunnits*
Like the brooch on her bust –
now she's on about sex lust

                          Is that the author?

We've read all his books
Imagined he'd have been
aesthetic handsome –
just like Jake in *Rogue's Passion*

Pens at the ready
we take down each word
how he spent a year
on a bender two as a road mender

                      Have you been published yet?

LUNCH! Not quite ready?
Lee come round the garden
see the view of the sea
air fills with technical jargon

Deadlines P.L.R.
rejection slips comps
royalties manuscripts
Have you read *The Bride Keepers*?

At three ninety nine
it's really a bargain
by Melanie Thring
same author wrote *Fate's Foundling*!

BUFFET'S there – turn right
Take a glass – red white?
Hostess is so kind
'Please do look at my study'

All paid for by
Glittering Bodies

That's my new novel
waiting for copies
processing posting
crowd round in awe at the door

Red cheeked and replete
fight for front row seat
new friendships have bloomed
past successes related

Is that the
Publisher's rep?

Can't be a day older
than Katie my daughter
dressed London Fashion
tan from Corfu Breadline's next's

called *Born In A Hovel*
by our author Joyce Brown
(Angel Dark's her by-line)
set in the foundries where love

knows no boundaries
Clog shod Annie runs
from her step-mother Grannie
without wardrobe or money

Boards a ship for New York
meets dissolute Lord
marries for money
has daughter called Wilde Honey

Goes on to become
head of a Company
called Dream Directoire
selling scented lace peignoirs

Hands up all owning
word processors?

Confessions follow –
publisher's rep says
can't guarantee that
editors will read *typed* M.S.S!

Pen has ground to a stop
own romantic novel
a guaranteed flop
TEA – minds are in overdrive

Meet author – charming!
In fact one of us
Leave before questions
inspired to begin novel

About Virginia
from wrong side of tracks
falls in love with boss
of local sweet factory

Called
Confections Of Sin.

'Goodbye till next year'
we run barefoot down
the driveway there's the
husband again waving us off

We sigh heavily
wishing own spouses
would run our houses
build workspace wash cook dinner . . .

then perhaps we would
top the R.N.A.[1]
spot – to our hostess
organiser friends
thanks a whole lot for super

brill Writers' Day
October '90

[1] *Romantic Novelists' Association.*

Blown Off Course

Seven years since self-steered *Warrior Queen*
slipped her moorings and I stood abeam
after jettisoning life's debris –
setting sail single-handed for life alone

Logging time speed high frequency signals
of distance route family friends and love
Beating to windward broaching to halfway
recovering to run before trade winds
twisters riding gales sleeping through calms

Driven on by ambition urgency
expediency programmed in my skull
keeping Sir Francis' warning 'don't look back'
as I sailed my personal Cape Horn

Now *Warrior Queen* lay becalmed sails limp
my hands healed long since resting on tiller
bones aching with sea-miles' longings for home
salt cracked lips moving in silent prayer

Sea birds quartered cliffs and I smelt autumn fires
heard throb of diesels as boats entered harbour
Suddenly my heart surged as a lifeboat
magnified across flat water closing

on *Warrior Queen's* bows throwing a line
welcoming me back I leap into arms
strong and sure – abandoning seven years'
lone voyage settling for life ashore again

Clampitt

Terror stalked Teign valley
dressed in a cloak of papist red
and believers abandoned steeple
house for Elias Tuckett's
stone farmhouse

Tranquillity under a cruck
framed roof filled puritan
hearts and minds stalked
by shadows selling freedom
for a bribe

King's men threw Elias
and his Friends into pestilential
jails hung others by the neck
shipped more to penal servitude
among rotting meat and plague

till a royal change of heart
set all Quakers free to worship
unmolested and bury their dear
departed nearby on Elias'
farm estate

Now walkers tread spring
snow flower paths and pause
at length to read

'Quaker Graveyard
1674 – 1740
Clampitt'

Live Now Pay Later

Airwaves carry an announcement
'Credit cards available
in Outer Mongolia'

Live now pay later has travelled
the Silk Road from the West
to land once ruled by Genghis Khan

Climbing turret by turret
a Great Wall built to
keep out Mongol hordes

where bicycle or honeymoon tours
can be arranged courtesy
of China Bank's own credit cards

Plastic squares fall
in a sleight of hand
for Cossacks at Ulan Bator

available too in antique
and friendship shops to buy
tourist tat and object d'art

Western make-up dress
brought in by World T.V.
replace Mao boiler suit cheongsam

Yet still tourists come
and walk without fear
for their personal safety

A cascade of promissory
notes fly ahead of storm hit
frozen tundra

Spring Sonata

Blue-green backdrops
a scene of virtuosity
arranged flowers scent
this sell-out musical event
conjured from
a borrowed Stradivarius
we listen

Brown curly head
nods in rhythm from a front
row seat his heroine
small distanced in years
demonstrates the
wider gap between his first
cello lesson her musicianship

Now he shares with
adults who once tortured notes
from violin strings
a display of dazzling perfection
we throng our local hall
spellbound packed in rows
to listen

She may never
come this way again pass on
entertain Europe's
heads become an international
name on lists
available on digital tape
and compact disc

This Spring brings
her blossoming soft skin
bare of make-up
brow furrowed she concentrates
solves a musical matrix
with small neat hands which stretch
and curve in performance

Coax cadenzas
from manuscripts written long
since in Germany
red taffeta dress fixes music
girl and time
Beethoven's Spring Sonata
Nicola Loud April 1992[1]

[1] *BBC TV Young Musician Of The Year 1990*

Catch Toe Click Click Click

Sunday and cars
stream through iron gates
spilling their contents
on grounds where weekday
children play

Punters search among
cast off clothes
broken pots from broken homes
souvenirs of sunkissed tours
green copper kettles
from better off days

Parachute silk
left from Grandpa's War
books on heaven, videos of hell
marching elephants
an old ship's bell
A pair of clogs
black leather uppers
with red stitched tops
fifty nails fix wooden soles
'rubber bottomed
for Sunday church'

Painting a picture
of poverty ridden dawns
in cobbled streets
competitions for pints of beer
sides of beef for families

Cotton mills turning
warp to weft translated
into clog dance steps
shuttles hum hands to sides
double beat step flick
catch toe click click click

Colours of Freedom

Black for the people
Green for the land
Yellow for the gold

Xhosa Govan walks barefoot
six hundred kilometres from home
press ganged by a mining truck

Signs his freedom away
with a thumb print on a list to work
underground in heat and dust

Marrying Selima
servant to a Kruger family
Wednesdays alternate Sundays free

When she dances nearby
in a chanting stamping tribal ring
to preserve her native identity

Black for the people
Green for the land
Yellow for the gold

Selima lives in a hut
by Karen's family swimming pool
and seven roomed house in Johannesburg

Supporting her children cousins aunts
who live in a barren rural town
where green land has turned to dust

Forced to absent parenting
her husband prisoner of a white regime
for believing in equality

Pinning hopes on Mandela
their constant hope and light
of inheriting a stolen native birthright

Black for the people
Green for the land
Yellow for the gold

Beneath their feet – Govan
takes home cash T.V. jeans other white trash
on six monthly visits to his tribal family

The Last Bastion

I press my nose on toughened glass,
search crammed shelves through dust and rain,
spot *The Old Devils* in hardback,
affordable at last.

A sign seals cracks between swing doors
leaking a musty leather bound
first edition smell – a 'phone
abandoned on the floor

No longer hums with requests
for Thomas, Clare, Dickinson,
the second line from 'How sweet
the moonlight on these banks'.

'*The Sea The Sea*' a novel
of genius for ninety pence,
The Heart Of The Moor by
convalescent Beatrice Chase.

A great place to spend wet days,
taste an expert's fungi in the fall,
track down a half remembered
phrase, remaindered books

Stretch black and white wall to wall
The words 'Closed Forever' cause me
real pain – never to come here
to browse again

Among '*Other Men's Flowers*'
collected by a desert rat,
nudging copies of Winston's War,
'Goodbye to all that!'

Widdershins

When we returned to Devon in 1972
traffic travelled widdershins
against the natural flow
history men dug Saxon pits
paved the way with ready mix
watched the traffic grow

Plane trees no longer shaded
our ancient market square
where wives sold butter – cream –
pullet's eggs – pigeon pairs –
curly kale – frosted sprouts
straight from the ground

People marched but all to no avail
sheep were penned beneath a multi-
storey – local crafts and bric-a-brac
were swapped for modern chain
stores till Newton Abbot
resembled Milton Keynes

Next came a brick built Berlin Wall
so cars could accelerate –
our brand new shopping mall
was opened by a Whitehall man who
scissored through red tapes
while traders remonstrated

but of course it was too late
soon it was hard to recognise
this fine old country town with
its rivers Teign and Lemon
banished underground – and
shops stared blank eyed

Next a Grade II listed coaching house
was sold to a consortium
who sold it to a developer
based a thousand miles away
disembowelled it stands
empty to this day

Progress raced on apace in spite
of local anger and debate – next to go
a park with swings and swimming pool
– this time the law was sought
but a loophole brought defeat – a plaque
marks the battle of Keyberry Street

and in their place a supermarket
to match one the other side of town
with petrol pumps and traffic layout
so one can cross the roundabout –
a relief road runs through cob and thatch
behind what was our market square

Plans to pedestrianise the main street
were submitted every year
but before they could accomplish this
they'd blitzed bus station – where
its site spawns government offices
built in a concrete monolith

But at last they've found a solution
for the problem's pressing now –
they're to make a proper job of it –
bulldoze remaining buildings down
settle once and forever the traffic
flowing over us widdershins cross town

Winter Passing

Cars carry us to Woodland's 'Rising Sun'
We wrap against cold winter's grip
crack ice on hoof cut bridle paths
wade water leaked to lanes from flooded fields

Booted feet slip on frosted waymarked stiles,
tread farmers' strips through winter corn,
skirt fields where pheasants rise across
a hinterland recorded in The Domesday Book

Four knights are listed in Broadhempston Church,
held ranks of cloth, a smell of incense
fills the parlour at the 'Monk's Retreat'
and walkers eat beside the village cross

Stone barns rounded under sheets of iron
where horses powered stones to crush
ripe orchard fruit men drank cider
where snow flowers group on boundary walls

Sheep flock together where we walk – we stop
for one white violet agree
among ourselves on Winter's passing
that it's late February and almost Spring

Childproof

Our third
and suddenly
I become childproof,
resistant to tiny fingers,
dimpled smiles.

Other people's children
can't win me,
can't reach me.
'Ugly little thing'
I think, steeling myself
to stay polite.

But now I see
a composite of faces,
faces known and loved,
thought gone forever
but brought alive
once more
in his brown gaze.

He grips
my outstretched finger,
crows his way into my heart
and, defences down,
I become vulnerable to,
not proof against,
his childish charms.

Excess Baggage

Years on and my response
is automatic
and I brace myself
for yet another
encounter of the human kind,
hope this one won't be
full of stress, promise
myself to stay remote,
ration time, ignore needs,
stay landlady hard.

Check facilities,
finish just in time.
She smiles but not her eyes,
puts out a cooling hand
and before I know it
we're sitting side by side
'You don't want to hear . . .'
then tells me anyway –
a suicide, a death,
the urge to get away.

Ashamed I murmur
platitudes, explain
the best place to eat
show her on the map
'Go now, don't leave it
late! Our town's kind enough
to strangers but be sure
to be back here by eight!'
I bite back experiences
shared with other guests.

Next day we say goodbye.
I press a talisman,
my card, into her hand.
Her words, her story,
stay in my head. Rapidly
I strip the bed. Refill
the coffee jar. Wonder
is it meant that they
should come and leave their
excess baggage here?

Inchcoulter
(For Elizabeth Renier)

February and blossoms burgeon
on these knurled and twisted limbs,
scent hangs in clouds
where once Inchcoulter stood.

Its Cottage coach house home
where carriage horse names
'Lady, Captain, Ginger' still
graced the stable loft.
And there, beyond
this cherry tree,
one August day we met,
drank gin, ate sandwiches.

Felt words waft skyward
through summer heat
on an unexpected breeze,
and conversation
bounced along a row of beans,
tomatoes staked against
a southern wall, as we
sat close to a statued pool.

Then, she began to read,
pass on her skills,
made people come alive,
involved us in a loving tryst –
pounding horses raced a storm
to deliver mail – and she showed
us how to use nuances, phrases,
set to work for children
to read in bed,

Now it was our turn to read
out fumbling words
against a background
of flowering treasure
and this tree (leafy then
in summer measure)
as we struggled to climb
the literary ladder.

February again and we stand
upon this empty plot
still signed 'Inchcoulter'
remember all we gained
when she lived near.

Blame The Supermarkets

. . . for merging all four seasons
and turning them into one
giving me strawberries at Christmas
and everything under the sun
is available from Egypt and Chile,
California, Holland and Spain.
So I'm wearing shorts in February,
sweaters from Iceland in July;
cooking lobster in October
while I've waved local yoghurt goodbye.

Swapped Cheddar cheese for Ricotta,
dress my salad in *Fromage Frais*
while Frenchmen in Calais
eat clotted cream from Devon all day
and, when squid and french fries come along,
I wash them down with glasses of Bulgarian Sauvignon.

Please supermarket bosses listen,
restore my reason and
give me back my sense of season

. . . keep Spring for cabbage, salsify,
chocolate eggs and hot cross buns.
Confine strawberries to June and Wimbledon.
Harvest onions and apples in September,
and don't above all, don't, bring out
mince pies and crackers until December.

Memoing (Miming)

Half term and they drive up the ramp,
stop by protective railings,
apply their brakes and rest.
Angle heads towards Tom
as he activates the looms,

tells his grandmother's story
in thick dialect of the women
grouped and smiling on the end wall
of this factory room.

'A bell set off clatter of clogs
as they raced across stone floor
to the clack of racks of reels in rows.
Reminds you of industrial terraces?'

'Their fingers flew – inches away
from broken limbs – to feed the grabbing
greedy cotton machines.' He pauses
'Memoing out their lives with eyes
and lips all for a pound a week,
less a shilling for gaslight and steam.'

Tom switches off belts driving
temperamental steam machines named
Ethel, Madge, Irene,
and it's silence now
that hurts our ears.

Hands, eager to be off, swing wheels
away from protective railings
but, at my request, pause to brake again;
smile as I flash my camera
then race each other up the ramp.

The Final Shift

Blindfold the horses came.
Some ran, some stood their ground.
'I'll never forget the heat
from the horses' breath
as I fell beneath their feet.'

Jason looked up
'What happened, what happened then?'

'I came to, son, came to
to the rattle of nightsticks,
the sound of bricks
on riot shields.'

A miner looks out of the frame
pockets supporting heavy hands
charcoal and wash reflecting
the end of the final shift.

Jason studies the picture
where it hangs in the half empty
room. 'Why did you strike, Dad?
We've to do a project at school.'

Tom brushes a weary hand
across his frozen face,
'I've told you, son,
told you again and again.'

Irene attacks a pile of sheets
'strike pay for a family like ours
were thirteen pound a week,
so we stole key to Parish Room
and there baked gifts of meat.'

She pushes away a strand of hair,
hair a premature gray.
'Tell him, Tom, tell him
how armoured cars broached
colliery gate.'

Tom took up the tale
'We'd have starved rather than cross
picket line, and it was rumour,
rumour that khaki was turning to blue,
that sparked miners' rage.'

His eyes flashed as Jason
played on his computer game.
'We stood, stone solid,
stone solid before closed pit gate.'

His eyes filled now, body tense.
Irene hurried across the room.
Jason, bored now, edged towards the door.
'I'll be off, then' he said,
but neither of them heard.

The Gallopers

Gray towers soft against
an Exeter sky, conceal a tree,
an Epiphany tree,
clothing the Cathedral
in white candled light,

And in Solstice short hours
I search for the spark
to start this event
cross History's green
drawn to the Guildhall
by piped organ sound

Where the Gallopers prance
around and around,
nostrils flaring,
eyes brilliant and bold.
Children, hair streaming, cling
to harness of blue, red and gold

Their chargers flying in pairs,
rearing and bucking
to old seaside airs.
Brass poles twist in a bright
burst of sun and flags fly
from a striped awning above.

Mirrors, beaded and bevelled,
flash and reflect
marionettes playing trumpet and drum,
while grandmothers clutch children
who came to see Santa
but ride the Gallopers instead
and shout out in glee

'Christmas, Christmas,
Christmas has come.'

Flood

Sara heard a sandbag hit her step,
remembered,
called in Ginger out preening in the yard,
made tea in flasks, sliced bread.
Moved photos of Stan in battledress,
Kevin and Kim in trim schoolwear,
dragged a mattress down the narrow stair.

It was a cloudburst late that afternoon
tipped the balance, caused the Lemon
to swell, drown peat bog and heather,
roar down the Sigford valley,
submerge ancient bridge and ford,
hang grazing sheep in willow forks,
set mill wheels creaking.

At sea a spring tide built beyond the bar
surged in past Teignmouth's Ness to
smash pleasure boats against the Quay,
race under Shaldon Bridge, slap river banks,
destroy kingfisher nests, lift herons
to rise high above the railway
and shelter in the trees.

Sara waited till she heard the slap
of water as it swept along her street,
watched salty sludge slide
under her front door to cover flowered
carpets, reach old marks in the hall.
Then, grabbed Ginger and retreated
up the narrow stair.

The two rivers met in Bank Street,
swept shoes from drowned shop doorways,
poured past The Globe to breach
Queen Street and Courtenay.
Douse fires in baker's ovens,
set free a grand piano to dance
back across the market square.

Ginger cleaned mud from his coat.
Sara pressed firemen to sandwiches and tea
while the moon rose over Newton, where
an eerie silence filled the air,
showing Bushell Ward and Bradley
once again divided as they'd been
in 1673.

Victim Support

They say
'You're mad to keep
an open house,
share with strangers,
pretend today's
the same sane scene.'

And afterwards

They said
'You only have yourself
to blame.'
But then they didn't share
the pain of precious pieces
gone to buy a fix.

And when I walk
beyond the tracks
to glean the seasons as they pass
they say,
'You're asking for it.'

And afterwards,

Would they shrug and say
'She only had herself to blame.'
Refuse to help,
retreat behind locked doors
into the bleakness
of their hearts.

Final Account

Coming to terms,
absenting strong warm hands,
sorting, sifting,
drawing up stray strands.

Checking customer
wedding orders,
cards enclosed by
deep black borders.

Searching upstairs
among his things,
ash dusted desk top,
autographed coffee rings.

Smoothing out creases
in folded down pages
where a magus conjured
credits, debits, wages.

Ringing up memories
on an ancient cash machine
as out of date
as his last campaign.

Cold smoke brings tears,
flames lick a long held brief,
consign the past to
a balance sheet of grief.

Bournvita For Two
(Forces Sweetheart Exhibition, Imperial War Museum 1993)

. . . in a honeymoon bed, not champagne
on a hotel bill, a khaki tunic on the floor
entwined with a shiver of caminicks
made by a WRAF from net curtains
the night before . . .

This ad in a Sunday magazine
draws me onto a London coach when paper
boys are still delivering. I brave
a bomb hoax, walk Westminster Bridge
pass 'Big Bertha' and on
into the War Museum.

A lump forms quickly in my throat
as I read battered letters in copper
plate from gas filled trenches.
A lump that grows as I view a soldier's
pouch of leather holding a baby shoe,
a smiling portrait of a shingle
haired young woman.

Anger replaces tears as Sam swanks
of conquests in a Flanders village.
Emily sends love, spelt out in black
suddenly switching to red, the day
his philandering comes to an end
in a shell hole full of mud
and rats.

I move on pass gas masks, campaign ribbons,
gold epaulettes, white feathers,
to a letter marked 'missing in action'.
Attached is a black bordered missive
from his commanding officer
promising a posthumous
V.C. instead.

Abandoning horrors from Hitler's war,
and 'the war to end all wars'
of twenty years before,
I go down a slope into a trench.
The feel of it I'll always
remember.

    Gas smoke urine blood excreta
    fraught with fear as poised
    on a firing step men wait
    for the officer's whistle.

I shut off my senses,
blot out the smell of cordite,
the crump of shells,
think of the Uncle I never met
the one who, to me, will
always be twenty.

Fabergé

Slowly we circle glass octagons
in a dimly lighted hall and I think
of Russian Winters when nights lasted till
ten next morning from three the day before
and Trotsky talked revolution, then fled abroad.

Russian music, sombre as Tolstoy's
'War and Peace' swallows us at the entrance
door. Blown up photos of Tsars, Kings,
and delicate plant designs
for jewellery fill the walls.

Elgar's 'Crown Imperial' establishes
the British link reinforced by enamelled
photo frames of Tsar Nicholas and George the Fifth;
cousins dressed in sailor suits, bearded, they stand
like twins by dairy sheds at Sandringham.

I admire a silver samovar, but have to wait
for the fabled egg. See cutlery taken to
a 'different' Siberia on Royal Summer trips
while grain crops failed and Russian workers
marched, and shouted 'Give us bread.'

War came and Fabérge's factory stopped
making gew gaws for the Tsar.
changed to hand grenades instead.
The German sounding St. Petersburg became Petrograd;
still Krapenskaya danced and Chaliapin sang.

Women workers faced the Cossack terror in July,
then Winter snows and revolution came on fast
and Russian troops, brainwashed by Isvestia,
changed sides, deserted Allied battle-lines
as Bolshevik 'truth' quickly turned to lies.

At last I gain the glass, see Nicholas's gift
to Alexandrovna in true Fabérge tradition –
an egg of gold with a surprise concealed inside.

As a child my father told me how to win the war.
Germany sent in a train with Lenin sealed inside.

Soon Tsar Nicholas became 'Comrade Tsar',
and found wanting by his people, was shot
in a lonely basement, his family by his side.
His son, a haemophiliac took longer to die,
Anastasia, it's said, was clubbed to death.

Sobered by the past, dazzled by porphyry,
enamel, jade; I drink coffee in the exhibition bar.
Recall the night the Berlin Wall was smashed
and democracy for Russians
arrived at last.

The Desk
Helen Glatz
Composer d.1995

. . . sits against the studio wall,
gold timber dark with age,
awaiting knotted hands
to come to rest, heavy
on the writing slope.

Phrases, themes, cadenzas,
lie pigeonholed against the muse,
burning to be used, seeking arousal.
Fingers seize a pen,
shake out larksong
in splashes of black ink.

Notate striated wings
to brush against the studio glass,
fly a canvas of summer light,
reach the upper atmosphere
to trill on strings and hover there,
a speck of black.

Drawers warped with the weight
of manuscript, pour out seasongs,
folk tunes in three four,
a city symphony,
a serenade for orchestra and voice.

Hands sift and sort grained harmonies,
drum out rhythm with fingertips,
stop to orchestrate the bird
earthward on cloudcapped wings
to nest among moorland heath.

And we, our spirits high,
watch the same fingers
close the desk
move across the studio
to try this fantasia
on waiting contrapuntal keys.

The Reading

Welcomed to a hotel room –
twin-sets, chintz and coffee cups,
white co-respondent shoes,
yacht club blazers, chinking bracelets –
I look beyond into the bay.

'We', I wave at Mary, Claire, met
through writing circles
studied Shakespeare, Manley Hopkins,
Larkin, Keats (I pause, wishing
I'd not begun this way).

I clear a drying throat, begin
a piece approved of by Greenpeace,
next comes *Rush Hour*, bang up to date,
then descriptive lines on Venice,
Sunday trips to car boot sales.

We three combine on country weekends,
wine, a sunless holiday in Tuscany,
end with *Reunion* which gets a laugh
followed by polite applause
and then, they come towards us.

I hold my breath, what reaction
to expect? Demands for books lying
in a pristine pile perhaps?
Requests for autographs?
Surreptitiously I reach for a pen.

'The street you mention in that piece
about a family.' 'Yes?'
'I know the woman who lives at No 63.'
She beams then fades while others
finger books. Our hostess
says

'I'll buy your book, but not today.'
Hesitates, then blurts out 'What I really want
is you to read *my* work, it's prose
but all my own. Or,
just tell me where to send it!'

Arrivals

I waited all through April
when dull days depressed my spirit
river mist masked Haldon's hills
and traffic torched its way
across the town.

She, Gemini and rebel,
cheeky, talented, a loving fidget,
had set herself new goals,
made me a special
promise.

And so I waited, while cherry
blossom lit up gravestones
on Wolborough Hill,
and listened for Spring's
herald.

Could green-radio yet be wrong,
crops stay uncut from under
nesting birds and set-aside
see nature's balance
once more restored?

Still no message came until
the end of May. Just when
I'd given up all hope of Spring,
house martins soared above
on swept back wings,

checked housing, and conversed
in high pitched screams.
Encouraged, again I walked the hill
and there it came cool, clear,
unmistakeable, across fresh flowered
fields. Confident, brash and
full of cheek – *cuckoo*

an omen perhaps?

I didn't linger, but ran
to claim the message
on my answerphone;
'A Gemini called Theo
with her delicate tapering
painter's fingers.'

Crystal Palace 1851–1936

(Inspired by Victoria's Albert and built to house the Great
[Industrial] Exhibition in Hyde Park, then removed to Upper
Norwood. Described as 'the fresh air suburb out of the reach of
valley fogs')

Sundays, then, we climbed a hill
at Havering-atte-Bower
to see the sun reflecting
primary colours from
flashing crystal towers.
Older now I tread the site
of parallel polygons,
find only Egyptian sphinxes
guarding mile long
empty terraces.

See people of mixed race
stroll where men from Rotherhithe
and Bow took part in cricket,
archery; wooed Sunday sweethearts
on a boating lake, and children
rode Professor Owen's
Plesiosaurus, Iguanodon,
nightly in their dreams.

Ada longed for a 'mehogany' whatnot,
a box of Sheffield plate.
Bands and fountains played
until a workman's cigarette
caused a conflagration more spectacular
than any staged event, reduced
my childish fantasy of wrought iron
and crystal glass into fused lead.

Now I stare across London's arc;
relive days in typing pools,
nights promenading concerts,
search the horizon for that
high Sunday viewing place

The End of The Affair

It is not you I miss
although you held my days,
it is the shape of hours spent, that's changed;
the time I have where once there was none left.
I fought for space and won, but now must pay.

Our time together holds me in a backward glance,
the pain of loss too great for tears
turns back the clock to other partings,
all bound up in acts of love.

We stay polite, pass gifts from holidays,
no longer share Swiss chocolate, French wine,
or a lover's kiss.

No Doom Or Gloom

. . . she'd said in that positive way she had,
a way of instilling hope in all who shared
her thoughts, a voice that wrapped one round
with warmth.

'That party will be for you. I want there
to be lots of touching, hugging, enjoying
food and wine, good conversation,
getting in the party mood.'

We did as we'd been told – shared memories
with families, put faces to friends
and colleagues who, until today,
had just been names.

Tried her knack of turning a sandwich
in a bar into a five star lunch, a rain ruined
holiday into fun, as sparky as Judy striking
Punch. A Sunday conversation on the telephone
would leave one feeling higher than the moon . . .

And so we drank and ate the buffet food
without a sense of grief, just huge relief
that all her pain was gone. Tears put on hold
we hung onto her brief, not admitting to each other
that life could never ever be the same.

Yellow
(Impressions of a visit to Berry Pomeroy Castle)

Yellow reflects the April sun
mirrored in drifts of bright kingcups,
watered by the Gatcombe mere
and a lizard basks on a fallen oak
close to a Castle's mute mill pond.

Ruins stand, stark silhouettes,
pillaged by villagers long ago,
built by Henri de Pomerai and used
as a setting for Edward Seymour's
refuge from intrigues at Court.

I study roofless walls pitted
with joist holes, blackened grates,
read information boards which tell
me how Sir John Soane built a copy
of Seymour's house in 1812 Italianate.

Bells ring in my brain, of course,
John Soane's house is now a museum
in Lincoln's Inn. I forget statuary,
artefacts, his drawings, bound vellum,
remember only drapes of yellow.

Yellow silk that sent me roaring home
to paint the same warm colour
on the walls of my own small sitting room.
Christine and I discuss this deja vu,
how Edward Seymour, Duke of Somerset,

Lord Protector, employed four hundred men,
built in London, Wiltshire, Bedford,
and here in Devon. Imagine the sun
that shines on us today shone on
Edward's execution on Tower block.

We pause, descend deep dungeons
where a sister languished in the cause
of jealous love, then search in vain
for Margaret's ghost. I climb a walkway
to the roof, look down on ramparts

where mailed and mounted brothers
jumped together to their deaths;
a cold wind brings the taste of blood,
a stench of night visitors
fills the air.

Message To My Mother

. . . and still I long and long to know the words
you wrote me fifty years ago. Wrote and sent
that Christmas tucked inside a handmade bra.
If only they'd been kept, not thrown away unread.

My careless act has haunted me throughout my life;
now forces me back to childhood days. I seek out
the album with its faded sepia print. The family
group dressed in our best with fishing rods
crossed over childish nets. You wearing
a proud smile beneath a dark cloche hat.

That day we trawled the lake, oblivious of what
was to come, the lost battle for your mind
against a background of cavalry mown down by tanks.
Dad's tears and workplace blown away by bombs
while, labelled, gas masked, I rode a train.

I turn the pages, there in black and white
stands Lizzie Chapman, my suitcase in her hands.
'Come along my dear,' she says, and leads me to a cottage
over threatened sun-baked fields, wraps me in her family
who fill my empty room with photographs,
    her son on leave
from training sorties over France,
    her daughter, my friend.

No-one came for me that Christmas as, dress pulled tight
by growing breasts, I undid your package to find
a handmade bra, and tucked inside a sheet of verse.
Now, hot with shame, I remember how I hid your words
from Lizzie Chapman's kind enquiring gaze.
'It's nothing – just wrapping.' I think that's what I said.

I close the album return to my self elected task.
Is this your hand now guiding mine?
Your mind which sends fresh images?

Snake, Toad, and The Long Crippled Grass Snake
(Leechwells, Totnes)

Chain mailed figures, white surcoats
crossed in red, kneel beside the rail to celebrate
a victory over desert infidel,
unknowing the legacy brought back by sea –
respecter of neither man nor woman, high born or low
– a bacillus eating limb or face.

Bell sounds warn the town beware the one
who hobbles, crawls on stunted limbs,
caped and gowned in black hood drawn tight
about a hairless sunken, ulcered face;
the husky voice escapes through wasted lips
'Alms, alms for pity's sake.'

At Leechwells the figure stops, looks about,
implores the Gray Lady of the Wells to cure
his ills, chooses between the three stone sinks
then stoops to bathe his tortured limbs
in Snake, Toad, Long Crippled Grass Snake,
then retraces his steps to Maudlin's Halls.

Come holy days, eight lazars leave the hospital,
process along the Leper's Walk,
take turns to peer through Mary's Chancel squint
to see a Crusader receive the wafer, host, from
a Holy Priest, while all the time they clutch
a leopard lily[1] to their throats.

---

[1] *Leopard Lily (fritillaria meleagris) or lazar's bell from its likeness to
the small bell a lazar was forced to wear to warn of his approach.*

Valentine's Night

. . . and the snow came thick and fast,
muffled traffic sound, painted terraces
with a mask of white,
laid down a carpet on the hill.

Next day a secret population was betrayed
by padding paws, running, hopping claws,
brushmarks made by tails
marking garden path and wall.

I put on boots, crushed sparkling crystals
underfoot, broke icicles from catkined
hedgebanks by the path to church,
gasped at the picture hanging Breughel-like
above the town.

Squat figures glissading down;
red cheeked, raw fingered, they laughed.
Dogs barked and ran about. Tall figures came,
dragged sledges up the field, reclaimed their youth;
hurtled down beneath a sky of icy blue.
A small boy rolls in ecstasy, head-over-heels,
head-over-heels, then stuffs his mouth with snow.

I tear myself away, slip through the churchyard gate
where daffs sag beneath soft weight, then brush free
a rose red heart tagged with messages of love,
and a silent robin guards a sweetheart interred beneath.

Images of Spain

At ten we leave Granada for Seville –
city tenements for a sunflowered plain.
A black haired woman takes the space beside me
till we reach her stopping place. She treads
an unmarked track to a hacienda where eucalyptus
gives shade, and men shake ripe fruit from olive trees.
The plain fills up with grazing herds;
black bulls for men to fight in Picasso's ring.

Next day we leave behind packed city streets,
walk past brown velvet goats near Monachil.
'Ola' a young boy calls, as we climb hills,
find space to sleep, a place to eat ripe apricots.
We're invited into a village bar to drink cold beer,
while outside a tethered donkey staggers in the heat.

Winter On The Prom

Sun splits cloud. Paints the horizon
with a silver edge. Gulls hang motionless.
Mufflered, Tom leads Dexter across the beach
where in Summer he'd be banned.
Both race towards a sandstone wedge,
watch yachts fight a five knot tide,
see clay boats hover at the bar and
locals fish for salmon on the slack.
Gray seas attack, lick ice cream posters
off the hoardings on the pier, and facia signs
in blue and pink dedicate a railway
gouged from sea and cliff.

A love meter sulks behind locked glass.
I long to press in a coin which heats my palm.
'Please tell me what the future brings?'
Dexter lifts his leg, Tom shrugs, points
to an early wallflower on the Prom, says
'There's always hope in Spring.'

By Request

No flowers
for one who knew the scent
of Dame's Violet in the hedge.

No psalms
for one who could tell
a Marsh Warbler from a Sedge.

No friends
for one who had at least a score
but, wanting to die alone,
banned them at the end.

No ritual
except the man of God, his wife
and I who knelt, ignoring her requests,
committed her to God against
piped organ sound.

We turned to go
and there she was beside me,
climbing an upland tor
pausing to claim the view.

Garden

Moss bound as a Devon wood,
gloomy as a graveyard
with its austere Victorian look,
wrong side of the track.

Battered by winds from the Teign,
Easterlies rape ripe shrubs,
shaded by clay brick terraces
bereft of sun, and back-to-back.

April brings a fleeting gleam
aslant a gap in granite walls
to creep at will, make its way
through my kitchen door.

Deck chairs lurk with spiders,
sleeping butterflies, rusting tools,
wait with me for June then, sun high,
emerge to work among Spring blooms
and I, in an old straw hat,
clutch coffee, book and cat,
move determinedly
from patch to patch.

Teenager

You wear your mascara
like a flag of defiance;
I shout at black fringed
baby blue eyes.

You toss thick brown hair;
rock the family car
as you slam the door.

Tripping in blue split skirt
on forbidden heels down
corridors, making dents

In masculine hearts, authority,
floors. Sweeping up hours
in a hair salon

Experiencing work,
then, riding a motorbike
with a boy called John.

Those earrings – disgusting
your Dad says, but you just shrug,
shooting cheap crescents

Up towards the stars and moon.
Firmly lock the bathroom door.
Make a rainbow head.

We exchange looks, bite tongues
dreading the moment you carry
our hearts through the door
for the very last time.

Hallo Old Woman

Her voice floated back,
a child with a thick
brown plait, skipping
past me on the stair
steps free as zephyred air;
no-one else was near.

My heart beat in time
to her youthful dance
remembering
a time I looked fair,
body light, hair bright,
holding dreams of chance.

But though my years span
six and three – her words –
'Hallo, old woman'
can't mean me!

Country Weekend Blues

I've got those country weekend blues;
there's straw in my hair and muck on my shoes;
no bus, no gas, no proper loos

but a grand view of the moor
and a right of way past the door
which puts me in touch

    with the locals.

I've got those country weekend blues;
crickets chirp all night long,
dawn comes up like a gong,

tradition is law, and at the end of the day,
there's nothing to do
but go down to 'The Bull'

    and drink up real ale with the locals.

I've got those country weekend blues;
there's soft rain for my hair
and gallons of fresh air

if you're not downwind of the pigsty.
I ride out to hounds, dive head-first from my
horse,
break bones on hard ground,

    trying to fit in with the locals.

I've got those country weekend blues;
no bus, no gas, no proper loos,
but that right of way past the door

heading straight for the moor
through acres of mud, past recalcitrant bulls
to a fog hidden tor,

  and I've fallen in love with a local.

Woman's Place

1914   Posters grew on public walls.
A finger pointed *Your Country Needs You*.
She dried her tears and joined the queue,
packing shells, making guns, waiting
for front line messages to come.

1918   Posters grew on public walls
advertising 'Jobs for Heroes'.
She left her bench and joined the queue,
seeking advice from Government departments.
'Woman's place is in the home'.

1939   Radio channelled the message anew,
tanks fight cavalry in Eastern Europe.
'All men report to your nearest depot'.
Women are needed to pack shells, make guns,
wait for front line messages to come.

1945   Radio channelled the winning news,
three great powers have reached Berlin.
She left her bench and joined the queue,
seeking advice from Government departments.
'Woman's place is in the home'.

1966   Prosperity for the nuclear family;
average children number almost three;
public opinion says
'Your children need you' to run homes.
To put an end to latchkey children.

1986   Twenty years on the media says
            'Times have changed, industry needs you'.
            She dries her eyes and joins the queue
            for training workshops; public shares
            or benefit shoes. 'Is woman's place still in the
               home?'.

1990   New decade and a falling birthrate.
            'Women are needed, that means you'
            to stack shelves, wield tools, while
            New Age man cooks food, washes clothes,
            cares for children.

1995   Redundancies, and women become executives.
            Man nurses, cooks, and cleans the home.
            Shares the birth and care of children,
            takes his place with woman in the home.

The Pinger Bringer

Crisis came one Monday
when, deep in coffee and
chocolate biks, Trudie
was telling us about
her latest trip.

We sat, riveted,
clutching our rejection slips
as we went over the Niagara
in a barrel, ate french fries,
sorry, I mean chips.

Annie had had a wedding,
we walked the aisle
step by step, Suzie's
grandchild was next
on the list.

Menopause, sex, M.E.;
walks on Dartmoor;
London exhibitions;
opera; literary bits
from the Sunday papers,

the latest media hits.
Is that the time?
Good gracious! Our
chairperson banged
her fist –

Work? (long pause) – Oh that!
We chatted on – I've not
had time, what with
this and that;
timed readings?

Oh, has it come to that
– a timer – like for boiling
eggs and baking cakes?
Whose idea was that?
Maggie's?

O.K., it's a great idea
Maggie, and you shall
be the 'pinger bringer'
to help us reach the top
of Breadline's latest list.

The Reunion

I'd have known her anywhere.
She sailed into view – dancer's body,
neat face, dyed hair – an older version
of the girl we'd known who read
tea cup fortunes in office cups,
confessing now to subterfuge.

We ate spiced chicken,
slipped back into time-worn roles.
They talked and talked. I sat
and smiled, fall guy to everyone
else's jokes, while the new men
in our lives sat, beguiled

as we painted a scene for them
of Beryl, Doris and I – just eighteen –
full of sheer nerve and camaraderie,
tapping out plaintiff words, contracts,
legal briefs, on clacking type machines.
Longing for Friday nights at King's Hall

dances. Wearing the borrowed, ankle length,
New Look, make-up, inviting glances.
Flirting with gray flannel trousered boys
in navy blue blazers and old school ties
who came on trips to Dovercourt Bay
to play cricket or rounders on the beach.

Two empty chairs can't quench our joy
as years dissolve and we become once more,
the girls we were forty years ago.

Smoke Screens

Smoke screens
start early
when truth
proves fallible
and all we've
been taught
falls apart.

Morals mist over
when mothers say
'sometimes, dear,
it's kinder
to lie!'

and, given
the go-ahead
We do.

The Big Issue

He leaves a row of beds, early enough
to beg a light from the cleaning shift.
Dressed tidily, not easy when it's tough
to trade debts for journals, stop the drift
from parent flight, to street, to frantic fix.

He settles for a second high street patch,
hours on, bundle heavy, sales number nix.
She stops when he calls out 'lady got a match?'.
Flameflare lights desperate eyes, a three day beard.

She returns lighter to bag, journal and coin
Pass from manicured palm to street
wise hand.
Heels click away, soon others stop and buy.
Confidence grows, he shouts 'Read the Big Issue.
William Morris, poor man's hero'. Sells out,
leaves on a high for curry and lager.

Moving House

Papers say there's nothing worse
than cutting loose, exposing roots,
packing up and moving house.

Neighbours watch your sale boards rise
wish you well, others just stay mute
and papers say there's nothing worse.

Next on trauma-scale divorce
comes high, 'though some don't give a hoot
at packing up and moving house.

While I shout, swear and curse,
change from gentle Jekyll to Hyde the brute
as I pack up and move my house.

Death itself comes pretty close,
but still, the papers get my vote
when they say there's nothing worse
than packing up and moving house.

Temporary Resident
Here lies Betsy Myers born 1893 died 1992
Spinster of the Parish of Bell Broughton
temporary resident. R.I.P.

Betsy Myers, born Teg's Farm, Plover Hill
just north of Pen-y-ghent
walked Horton Moor to learn life's skills
milked cows scrubbed pails
baked best bread at Broughton show.
Grew up with feeling hands for all the creatures
on the fell. Nursed Alice and Bill
till they were dead.

Eviction came she packed Tom Watson's V.C.
from the Somme, moved south to Hebden Bridge.
Then war's done and mills closed she missed
her life on Plover Hill. Lined boots with headlines
packed Tom's medal, biscuit, tea and kettle
in a canvas sack. Called up the oldest dog
took to the road, split logs for money
begged for scraps.

Weathered now, as limestone walls on Pen-y-ghent,
she trudged south, always south, to find Tom's camp
on cratered cartridge ridden hills. Planned
how she'd spend her hundredth in a shaft of sun
where summer solstice hit key stones.
Tired at last she settled for a graveyard bed
laid a tender hand upon Jack's brindle back
'we'll stay the night.'

One Is Fun

'One is fun' she said
as she stripped the sofa bed,
packed hedgehog mugs, that dreadful sixties
lamp, making me a present of a recipe book.

'Here' she said 'this is for you. There's
a recipe for making "all-in-one pan"
a meal for a vegetarian. Then by adding garlic,
a dash of herbs, crème fraiche and wine it turns
into a cordon bleu for two.'

'One is such fun' she said 'no fighting
for the duvet in the middle of the night
and phone calls – why they're all for you.'
later I discover the bills are too.

'You'll never get sick' she said 'there'll
be no time for that' but when I am
and the pills run out there's only me
to put them back.

She went on 'I really can't emphasize just
how much fun there is in being one!' She sighed
with regret, handed me her 'how to'
library and left.

'How to mend the car,
change a fuse,
re-washer that nightlong dripping tap,
send off a fax,
slim from ten stone to eight,
reconstruct a rotting garden gate.'

Then it was that I remembered,
all too late, the day she told me
'One is fun', why, that was the day
she moved in with her boyfriend.

Mowing The Allotment

Cowslips cluster on motorway cuttings.
bellflowers bloom on burial plots,
strawberries flower on railway embankment
and it's time for cricket
and allotment keeping.

Curtains curve clean as canvas
old wives tales revive in
a wind from the East and it's time
to pay Council fees, defrost seeds,
for Sunday mornings of solitary peace.

Madge musters her late requests
'more earlies, less beans, please Jack.
Oh, and straw flowers for my floral art.
don t forget redcurrants and raspberries
for my summer tarts.'

Jack sighs, shrugs, tamps tobacco,
mentally makes space for at least
one prize marrow, cleans fork and spade
pumps tyres, loads trailer, adds at the last
forbidden mags, a handmower to cut the grass.

Yes, it's time, although late this year,
time for wicket and allotment keeping.
bats snick balls to silly mid-on, spades
attack cold soil till Jack gets on a sweat,
breaks out his cache of home made beer.

Drinks a toast with his neighbour, Fred
says 'Here's to England and success.'
Shines up the windows of his corrugated
shed, settles inside for a smoke, a sleep
to dream of the summer which lies ahead.'

Down To Earth

Josh throws the first clod
hits little Amy squarely between the eyes,
A communal gasp explodes from adult throats,
then, they take sides, line the allotment,
seize clumps of steaming dung

Take careful aim, fling with all their might
till straw and rotting turds
cling to hand knits, shaved heads,
beaded locks and, thus encouraged,
kids follow their parents' example.

'This is not what our allotment's
supposed to be about'. Leader Jane protests
as cheeks glow, minds and muscles find release
from stress as dung falls clod by clod
onto a square of newly cleaned sod.

'Harmony, healthy food, family co-operation'.
Jane's protest goes on and on
till Angie's aim fells her in one.
Over tea, brewed on Jake's fire of summer decay,
autumn detritus, Jane's good humour is restored.

'Let's do this again next Sunday!'
kids and parents exclaim as they fill sacks
with a harvest of parsnips, potatoes, pumpkins
and celeriac. Bikes are pulled from hedges
loaded with sacks and squashed through the gate.

Josh and Amy, friends now and last to leave
emerge from a den near the compost heap.
'Hurry Josh, there s Pasta Pesto and
Garlic bread for tea.' Satisfied at last
Jane smiles, firmly locks the Allotment gate.

Sensory Garden
(Presented by Action for Blind People to Teignbridge District
Council
Commended in the 1995 White Cane Award)

Because this garden
was not made for me
I shut my eyes and become blind,
like you, you for whom
this scented space was made.

Put my trust in feet
to find the way over specially
studded paths which skirt
a maze of aromatic herbs
and seasonal blooms.

Hands too become eyes ,
touch leaves, shiny as polished brass.
rub plants to release scent,
then wince as my fingers
are cut by jungle grass.

Other intruders have broken
into this dedicated sanctuary,
evidenced by this vandalised seat,
the bottled glass which rolls
this way and that beneath my feet

Sounds of children, barking dogs,
reach me across the park,
disturb my concentration and,
now exhausted by pretence,
I open my eyes again.

At once fear is dispelled,
fear which came in that moment
when I banished sight
Not for the first time, and I've been
here a score, I wonder why you, the blind,
are never here?

You, for whom this sensory space
was planned, to give you pleasure,
Invite you to bask among this scented
treasure. Perhaps it is that you too
feel vulnerable?

Or do you, the blind,
come at other times
and not alone?
Please tell me for I
Need to know.

Discovering Rock

Was this the boy who ran from screaming jets?
Spent primary years on igneous hills
swam battered sea caves, grew to the magnet
pull of mountain heights lure of glacier fields?
Climbed lung leeching volcanic slopes ice stepped
ladders, reached up to flag torn summits
where spirit messages from other cultures
fed back a magma of strength to commit

For use by boy now man, son now parent,
helped newly weak to cross time's scarp, love's scree,
built bridges above and below the heart's crust,
travelled the highway through Pakistan
observed life lived daily by the Koran
discovering rock, discovering man.

A Child's War

Leaving school at fourteen
all bust and flying hair
torn from my wartime family
bound for London
where night was full of obstacles
streets a pitch dark black
then it was that terror came
every night at six
with the warning wail of the siren
a sky criss crossed by searchlights
and the crack of the ack ack gunners
shooting from the park.

Leaving shorthand classes
to cycle a hop lined lane
Lil and I saw the dagger shape
of a rocket flying overhead.
The engine cut and, hearts thumping,
we threw down our cycles,
jumped into the nearest ditch,
then, breath on hold, we counted
and as our fingers reached to ten,
relief filled our bodies
because we knew
that we weren't dead!

Exile

Rumours travelled faster than the enemy
rumours of our women raped, our men killed,
our farms burnt – Father abandoned the harvest
loaded the horse and cart and left.

Three women sit, meal done, table scrubbed,
coffee made, language book between them –
Two search for words to tell the third
how they came here.

Brigitte speaks first,
a pulse throbs in her neck.
'Fifty years! Is it so long ago?
mother crying as we left, Sabine
had just been born. There was no milk,
a sheet became her shroud. Father used
a spade to break the frozen ground.'

She stops, her knuckles whiten
as she grips her coffee mug.

Grete begins to pace the kitchen floor,
a shaft of sunlight stipples wooden walls.

'I, oldest of ten, remember more.
By day we hid within the forest halls
and walked by night, heard shots –
our Fathers "don't look back!" Ten days
it took to walk to freedom's zone.'

Brigitte shivers in the heat,
lights up a cigarette.

'For years I dreamt of scabies,
woke to the feel of blisters on my feet,
lice crawling in my hair, dreamt
of the camps, the nightmare that was there.'

Grete takes down her graying plait
twists and twists it through her hands

'School here was bad – they called us
Hitlers, Nazis
Father laboured on a farm, mother exchanged
flour for bread – so we survived.'

Their pain is all too evident.

Joined to them by marriage vows
I take their hands in mine and
count my blessings, never
to have known of exile until now.

The Galway Hooker

Mist on the Maumturk mountains
had brought us here, past peat cuts
to coffee and re-plan the day's itinerary.

She, courier to a party of French
looked skyward in despair.

    'Two hours still to lunch!'

Together we read the dedication
on the lone marble slab.

    'On this site in 1897,
    nothing happened.'

She translated, both English and French
laughed.

    'Nothing's going to happen 1996'

Anne said, reading the sign on the workshop door.

    'Closed all day',

Cameras recorded the scene against
a glory of yellow gorse, rampant rhododendrons
reflected in the grey morning lake.

Siobhan smiled, a friendly Irish smile,
against jet black hair, eyes of
Ballyconeely blue.

'It's no good for the mountains.
Why not take the scenic route to Roundstone.
The Galway Hooker's there – if you're not
too late!'

'Too late for what?' we asked.

But by then she'd boarded the orange continental
coach and disappeared. With nothing to lose
we drove the twisting lake strewn road.

'Who do you suppose is the Galway Hooker?'
Anne asked 'Must we abandon our search
for the old Ireland for one for a velvet
furnished bordello?'.

'Disport ourselves before a two-way mirror
while Madam supplies a Brian Boru of a man
to make our "hands on" Connemara experience
truly unforgettable?'.

Gloriously harboured Roundstone emerged
from the gloom, houses lined with pot plants,
garden flowers, the Hotel with grand lilies,
a study of Christ's aura'd head, flanked
by a pair of candelabra.

Puzzled

'Is this a farewell (with message) to the
famous Galway Hooker' we said.

The waitress bringing coffee and soda bread laughed

'You've missed her, she's just left.'

'Left for where?' Anne asked. 'Has she
serviced this community and is travelling
on to the next?'.

'No, no' the waitress said 'It's Corpus Christi,
there's to be a procession, a harbour blessing
by the Priest, music in the Bar'

we registered excitement

'But not till after Mass.'

Months later, browsing Irish travel in my local library
I found a photo entitled

'Turf boat entering harbour,
the Galway Hooker, sails trimmed.'

By Patrick Donal O'Bryan.

The Other Day

I thought I saw you
the other day –
same look, same height,
same turn of the head

I thought I heard you
the other day –
same walk, same sound,
same lurching step.

I thought I touched you
the other day –
Same skin, same kiss,
same word unsaid.

Flash Red Car

Surprised at the change
from station wagon
to foreign flash car finished

Vermillion red, red that matches
the setting sun streaked over
a ceiling of winter amber

Amber that covers long shadowed
deeps both sides the road
between Dartmoor and Ex.

I, the passenger, look
over my shoulder to catch
the sun's growing death

While she, the driver, copes
with oncoming traffic
fast fading light.

Lowering my gaze, smile
at crumpled blankets in the back –
see again Bonnie, bold Moss, Wild Tag

Smell again that vintage
wine of dung, pony nuts
and binder twine.

Turning back to face the road
ahead I know, without a doubt,
that nothing has changed

Just the outside, from sturdy
station wagon to flash red car,
inside things remain the same.

Migrane

Travelling dark December
toward the shortest day
head pierced through by moondarts
aura'd round by crackling
emerald coloured glass.

Travelling dark December
passed blinding sunshot tracks
over exposed to solaroids
speech reduced from diction
to utter gibberish.

Travelling dark December
behind a black peaked cap
eyes shuttered by dark lenses
making morning journeys Westward
post meridian only to the East.

Departure

Evening and the sun paints
a red path across rounded hills
down, down, the river Teign
to reach the Estuary.

Reflections flash from cottage
window to fishing quay and our lad
joins others, excitement tangible
as each takes his leave.

Adventure awaits as they board
the 'Florimel' where she lies at anchor,
water slapping her twin hulls,
burgee jingling in a freshening wind.

We race over Shaldon Bridge,
set up camp at the Point, as close
departure as we can while his sisters
trawl for shells, pass bathing huts,

Jump lengthening shadows as the sun
goes down beyond Haytor and windchange
comes with tideturn and we're
drawn toward the sea.

We watch moonrise light the scene
as waves gather beyond the Bar
and roar across the Estuary,
beckoning man and boys on 'Florimel'.

We banish the gale warning firmly
from our minds as gulls swoop
across her bows and she leaves
the safety of the riverbank.

'There he is' the girls point
as we strain our eyes to identify
our lad among the crew, standing to attention
at stern, at helm, at boom.

'Bon voyage, good luck' we shout and wave
as 'Florimel' sweeps downriver,
leaves the shelter of the Ness,
makes for the gap within the Bar.

Fighting the tide race to breast
towering seas and is swallowed
up by the tide, the stars,
the moon, the sea.

Last Swim

The knot of fear
once more here
as a wave curves
into the shore,
sending an invitation
on rainbow-coloured spray
and I watch them running barefoot
into the sunlit bay.

Marooned on my picnic island,
I shield my eyes and search,
but bobbing heads all look the same
as they swim among the surf.
panic grips my senses
as I lie helpless on the beach.
do they know there's an undertow,
that a freak wave lies within reach?

Mouth dry, heart beating fast
I shut my eyes and pray,
till suddenly they're beside me
glistening and wet with spray.
their skins are cool to my hungry touch
as they tell me how good it's been
then eat as though they'll never stop
as I force hot tea through my teeth.

All packed up, time to go,
just one last, long, look at the sea,
knowing that next year
will find me
once more here,
dread time of year,
watching, watching the sea.

Physic Garden

Violet coloured
September berries
culled from Devon hedges
fermented fear
as well as wine.

She produced a tray,
bottle opener, glasses.

'Drink, darling,
it may do you good'.
She said.

He smiled, shook his head,
sat on, idle but content
as tools rusted,
hebes outgrew space,
spent flowers writhed
across his once neat lawn.

He pressed her hand,
eased his aching frame.

'Not yet, not yet
I'll know when it's time'
He said.

Scan No 6

Sonar rooms must be dark.
Sonar screens must be black.
Images must be wrought from the womb
by white mechanical cat.

There are no secrets in the sonar room.
There are no secrets on the sonar screen.
White coated operators see to that,
wielding jelly, callipers and probe
to measure and record and parents to be
must accept the professionals' report.

'Nil growth since Scan Number 5.
You don't want to know the sex?'

Parents decant these worrying words
in the consulting room.

'Growth dips and swells, don t worry
all will be fine.
Scan number 7 will prove.'

Meeting Ralf

Requested by the father-to-be to check progress
I find her alone – unravelling the age old
secret between mother and daughter,
outstretched her hand is irresistible.

Together we watch needles trace paper
patterns, heartbeats monitored on a screen
red for child, green for mother,
accompanied by a constant bleep.

Mountains are climbed, waves breasted.
Suddenly red light disappears from screen,
at first I freeze then run for help.
Ward becomes theatre, she bionic
attached to wires and drips.

Sucked out into a blaze of light
Ralf is tiny, undernourished,
but life is there in her bold blue eyes.
Cameras flash as her name is unrolled
And tried out. Rachel for herself.

Ann for a cancer victim. Louise for a great aunt
she will not meet. Frazer for a small woman
on a Scottish croft. Even allowing
for gaps her name measures more than she from
her topknot of hair to her long dancer's feet.

A Trick of The Light

. . . raises mast and square sail,
a row of warshields runs the length of each side,
horned helmets glint, norse backs bend
to the pull of the sea and a helmsman calls time
then suddenly sails burn, masts crack, flames envelop
the Viking invaders, swallowed whole
in the glow of the lowering sun . . .

Evening crowds stream down to the Harbour
to join an Armada heading out to Nut Rock
where 'Pettifox' waits to start the Gig Race.

Paul takes his place in blue 'Bonnet'
the oldest gig in the Islands of Scilly
proud to be chosen he strips to the waist.

Pistol crack and muscled arms strain
to pull heavy boats away from the line,
motors turn slowly in supporting launches.

'Men-a-vaur', 'Czar' row for Tresco and Bryer,
'Nornour' and 'Shah' for St Agnes and Gugh
fighting a nor'easter that whips up the ocean.

'Dolphin' blown from St Martins
fights off 'Serica' cheered on
as its bow passes the rest of the fleet.

Halfway and 'Eagle' challenges 'Dolphin'
then weight tells as 'Bonnet' approaches
slicing through the late tide into Garrison harbour
a ripple of muscles speeds past Rat Island
to a welcome hurrah for the winners

'Paul and his team'.

*'Pettifox' the Scillonian name for the five bearded
Rocking, an eel like fish good to eat. This 'Pettifox'
is a 36ft Gaff Cutter built on the lines of the Breton
Crabbers which used to fish around the Islands.*

First Timer

At last I understand
the look that separates
first timers from those
who've been before.
one woman every year
since donkey carts transported
mail, papers, tinned commodities
from ship to shore.

Then sea birds and fish
were fat and plentiful.

Patterned days evolve
morning departures
in a fishing boat converted
to the tourist trade.
Paul, sea young, wind blond,
navigates narrows, hidden wrecks
to show us puffin burrows on Annet
seal colonies on Eastern Isles.

Across the Broad 'Earthkind'
volunteers count sea grass
on the Atlantic floor
and herring gulls disappear.
Replaced by whirring,
vibrating rotor blades
flattening grass, slicing
through off island peace.

How long will Bryher, Tresco
keep their strings of amber
their silent pools
their seas of emerald?
Stay home to hunting peregrine,
strip farmed daffodil,
Bermudan buttercup,
granite walls host
Hottentot, aeonium?

How long the magic Scillies
hold the look that says
'I've seen the sun go down on Samson,
watched sea furies raging at Hell Bay
caught puffins fishing off St Agnes?'

How long will faces hold contentment
all voiced in that one short phrase
'Oh yes, I've been before.'

Those Hazy Days of Summer

When the temperature climbs
to a sizzling seventy eight
let's bring out the bar-b,
dress dead cazh and celebrate,
set match to fuel, heaped
on a home-made grate,
flame fan the glow
to two hundred centigrade.

Ignore summer's steamy languors,
bring out the marinade
and Dad's favourite bangers.
'Tom, better ask the neighbours in
– Oh and tell Gwyn the ginger beer's
not the same stuff that blew out
the windows of his garage last year.
better lace the elderflower with gin!'

'Jake, light the garden flares.
Tom, bring out a bucket of water.
Amber wipe the plastic chairs.
That cant have been thunder?
Michael Fish said . . .
That was lightning . . .
Oh, hell, here comes the rain.
Don't bother with that – just run!'

Liz Taylor's Eyes

Violet is the colour of lobster
before its Thermidor
shadows reflecting fresh falls
of snow, striped paintings
in Kunst Aus Zurich, the final
band of a beached rainbow.

Cloud coloured warning
of a thunderstorm,
cheap Devon scent,
posies sold by gipsies in City
Streets, a beloved aunt born
before the war

Plumping ostrich feathers
like a parakeet.
rays burning ultra from
the sun, mini-skirt draped
stool in my local bar.

Twilight – that time of day
between Happy Hour
and the evening star.
Liz Taylor's eyes.

'Kunst aus Zürich'
art from Zurich

131

Heligan

What a lark, eh Jack?' Tom said
as they left the Recruiting Office.
'Chance to see what's t'other side
Tamar Bridge!'.

Choice hadn't come into it
with pilchards all fished out
tin prices in Bolivia closing Cornish mines,
so Tom and Jack climbed uphill to Heligan
the Tremaynes' big house.

Faces unmasked, they sprayed
rows of vegetables and flowers
with those widow makers, arsenic
and nicotine, determined to defeat
the ever advancing weeds.

Seth, Head Gardener, sensing promise
promoted Tom and Jack to build
steaming tropical heat in dung filled
pits, produce melons and pineapples
for the pampered rich.

Night shifts spent stoking boilers
hidden behind blood red brick,
setting traps for scavenging rats,
day shifts braving bees to harvest
honey from the beebole skeps.

Then, stalked by a widow maker
called 'War' Tom and Jack signed
their names on the lavatory wall,
cleaned their tools,
hung them up and left.

Without Tom and Jack exotic fruits
shrivelled and died, hothouses grew cold,
silence fell on lawns and espaliered trees.
The Master of Heligan looked in vain
for his daily peach.

Eighty years on, rescue came
to the garden of Heligan.
Old tools emerged from the shed intact,
handles smoothed and worn by Tom and Jack
and their workmates who never came back.

*(Of the 22 gardeners who went to France from Heligan only half
returned. They are remembered on the War Memorial at St. Ewe).*

Lookalike

Hallo, Sylvia!' she comes towards me
arms outstretched 'How good to see you again!'.

I've never seen her before in my life
but, faced with such confidence,
hesitate a mite too long, am forced to sit

opposite at this poets' board lit by candles
of beeswax, eat vegetarian pasta, drink rough
Spanish red, nod occasionally at literary feats,
trying all the while to banish
my 'Sylvia-ness'.

Dinner over, we gather to listen as she
fashions words of country, coast and fishermen,
finishes with a fun piece on being a poet's wife.
Then, after applause and signing, she puts on
her cape and turns to go, hesitates,
casts one last long accusatory look
in my direction and asks

'Are you sure you're not Sylvia?'.

Workshop No 2

Jealousy

Barely perceptible
a nuance of speech
lift of brow
coolness of mood
promises are broken
you move out of reach
break each vow
life's eroded
with stifling suspicion
ashes for roses
bitter scent
imagined embraces
fears gain in momentum
filling empty hours
with regrets
and reproaches
till the heart
implodes into pieces
through the
pain of unknowing.

The Right Side of The Pier

Beneath the Pier perch Tom,
Young Jim, atop a barnacle laden beam,
their summer split – cockling on the Salty,
then climbing up the struts
beneath the Pier.

Sandwiched by the sand below,
the boards above, they listen to the children's
drumming feet as they race towards the rides
boat swings and dodgem cars,
above the Pier.

    'When I'm a man' says Tom
    'I'll play them penny pinball machines.'

    'And win that watch for me' Young Jim replies
    'you know the one – silver
    but with golden hands'.

The sun goes down, the moon comes up.
sea sounds change, waves grow and gather speed,
advance in dangerous leaps, attack the Pier.
too late to jump and run, desperate
they cling to their beam.

    'What if our Jack hadn't been out there
    collecting pots?'

Their Mother cuffs Tom around the ear.

    'From now on you keep Young Jim
    topside the Pier'.

Above the Pier lie Tom,
Young Jim, atop the rows of peeling
painted planks, their summer split –
cockling on the Salty – watching lovers
underneath the Pier.

'Tidd'n the same' sighs Tom
'I miss the shells, the crabs, the tide.'

'One day you'll win that watch for me'
Young Jim replies 'you know the one
– silver but with golden hands.'

The sun goes down, the moon comes up,
the sea advances on the Pier.

*(Read at the 1996 Teignmouth Festival by Brian Matthew
Actor and broadcaster).*

Rain In The Hills

(It was believed that a pregnant woman couldn't make butter).

Rivers, seas, harvested
by a searching sun,
fall as rain on an old straw roof
to fill gutter, butt and trough
where Prince slakes his thirst
then rests a foot.

Across the passage his master
lusts after the red haired
dairymaid who works the churn
prays the curd will turn
to butter, give the lie
to the old wives' tale.

Fresh clouds burst, swell bog
into stream, stream into rivulet,
boil and roar down Ter Hill,
skinsoak Jem working night-shift
at Hooten Wheal. Wet breached,
stripped to the waist he crawls

Streaming terraces, prizes tin
from the earth's largesse,
dreams of Tansy and the promise
he made after Whitsun Church.
Storm winds douse lamps,
drive rain beyond the mine
to fill the Skir Hill leat.

Agnes, farmer's wife, mixes
pastry made from beef and wheat
throws out spent rain
to stipple stones, gurgle along
gulleys, descend into drains.

Exhausted rain clouds
move east, leave a lazy shower
to fall, drop by drop, on Tansy's
bright hair as she pegs clothes,
dreams of Jem and what she must
tell when they meet again.

Red Earth

Brown fish hovered
mirrored in mottled stone,
water chinked, gurgled,
changed to a different note.
trout wriggled, dived,
warned by distant baying
in the snow flowered wood.

We straightened, waited,
watched him break cover
mud clinging to his flanks,
sweat dripping from his
lolling tongue as he ran
toward us down the bank.
seeing us he checked.

We froze, hopes high on rescue
from this trail of death
as he slipped into the Becca
then sank to a silent streak
swimming back the way he'd come.

We watched, counted
a forest of white tails,
yelping tongues, they much
larger than that other
outrun thirty to one.

We shouted, ran about to confuse
this death machine till Control,
heavy jowled in pretty pink,
thundered down, copper horn
rapping on his chest.

He swore, we hissed
escaping as black hunters
took our place. Later
we clutched our mourning drinks
remembering soft dusks
when a cub
he played on Bonehill Rocks.

Grey dawns meeting eye to eye
on Golvers Hill or, silent as a shadow
as he slipped through Sigford's
bluebell wood. White feathered mouth,
crossing cotton bog from Holwell Lawn
to Honeybag. Running free in a coat
to match red earth.

Ötzi

Cable car jerks us from Arosa's
skating lake to Weisshorn's viewing place,
such sudden ascent causes me
sickness and a blinding head.

Muesli laced with rum restores
my equilibrium and I'm free to enjoy each
snow-capped peak. Ferdi points 'Beyond
the Alp lie Innsbruck. Trieste and Turin.'

'Could I reach Vienna thru' the Pass?'
He smiles 'In July but only with a guide.'
Again he points 'Over there they found him,
the bronze age man sealed in a tomb of ice.'

Back home I find Ötzi in a magazine,
clothes and arrow-quiver made of deerskin,
cape and dagger-sheath of grass,
his reconstructed eyes surprised.

Science put his time of death 3,000 B.C.
suggest climactic change lured him,
a nomad, to climb beyond the trees
until, exhausted, he fell asleep.

Roots

Sometimes I think
of leaving when City roots
begin to pull
smell market streets
childhood parks
meet old friends in dreams
but then
autumn cyclamen bursts into bloom
leaves turn gold at edge of town
and I hang on await western gales
to bring an end
to summer's pleasures
visits from friends
who envy me this Eden place
its uplands soft seas stone strands
besides where could I go
to find my roots
family home long gone
perhaps it would be best
to wait
till Spring.

Rain On Tuscany

Storm rain fell on Tuscany
filled gargoyles, gutters,
streets, rattled on a bright
umbrella painted scene.

Shop owners scattered sawdust
on Naninni's tessellated floors
tourists lit candles in
ancient marbled halls.

We walked through Romulus's
gothic city gates and soft rain
still fell on ochreous clay.
Sage, thyme, thrift

grew by stone farms, guard
dogs ran the vineyard covered
hills. We listened to the day
song of a nightingale

till thunder sent us running
to shelter in a barn while water
clad the star shaped hills
and boots slapped mud.
Another day descending
Sienna's red brick stage where,
each summer, riders on rearing steeds
race for their beliefs,

a curtain raiser filled
the streets, small drumming
boys, men in slashed
scarlet sleeves

whirled flags round bodies
starting at hip, then waist,
then chest, then neck, flinging
flags high above the ring.

At night we walked reflection
studded streets, blotted out
rain sodden days with pasta,
wine and travellers' tales,

that May, when records broke,
and rain fell in torrents
on Tuscany.

PMP (1990)

February Starlings

St John's cross stands
proud of Saturday's grey town,
mast and hull lie becalmed
in the harbour below.

Sudden bird cloud arrests
our departure and we watch
its black flight swoop, dive,
gyre round street chimney and row.

Then flip over, breasts pale,
split in two, one group diving
seaward, the other climbing
a sunset streaked sky.

Formation tight they regroup
to dazzle us with close feathered
flight, confusing hawk hunters
who quarter the heights.

Finally ending this pre-roost
display the birds roll over,
looping-the-loop to drop dizzily
clipping rooftop and wire.

Settle at last on gargoyle,
cupola, ledge, while we listen
entranced as the birds
click, whistle and sing.

Preen glinting feathers
of purple and green, akin
to street boys getting ready
to go out for the night.

Workshop No. 6

Joy

Click, click
photos cover front page lives
genocide war torture death
but where is there joy?

Flash, flash
photos cover exhibition walls
starvation rape famine flood
but where is there joy?

A naked girl runs at Pnomh Pen
straight toward a camera lens
clothes and skin burnt from her back
her face a scream.

Seventeen years on
she faces Reuter U.S.A.
'I forgive you'
she tells the men
who threw the flame.

Scars concealed beneath a shirt
her lovely face serene
'I'm alive. I'm happy.
I'm free of pain.'
Phan Thi Kim is full of joy.

Lullaby

Lower me down the well of sleep,
through layer on layer of down soft dream.

Banish darkling fears from shadowed walls,
toe search cavities in stone stair wells.

Fly feathered hunters the dim hedgerows,
pen beast to byre, bring outings in.

Obscure the light, sing lullaby,
love heralds night, sweet sleep is here.

Otter (1989)